When Half of Your Heart Dies

by
Gloria Clark

PublishAmerica
Baltimore

First printing

ISBN: 1-4137-4494-X
PUBLISHED BY PUBLISHAMERICA, LLLP
www.publishamerica.com
Baltimore

Printed in the United States of America

In loving memory of my deceased family members:

Michael Wayne Hilliard
5/4/90 - 4/16/98

Catherine (Williams) Paris
6/14/34 - 9/6/91

Toyami Leverta (Clark) Paynter
12/8/62 - 1/6/98

Carolyn Ann (Williams) Shamberger
1/7/50 - 11/24/86

Tanya Elise Shaw
3/21/70 - 10/28/90

Bennie Williams
12/1/04 - 8/26/75

Latrice Lynette Williams
2/19/75 - 11/25/78

Spc. Michael Leon Williams
9/11/57 - 10/17/03

Omega Williams
4/5/1905 - 7/22/03

We Love and Miss You

Special thanks to some of Darian's many special family and friends whom he loved so deeply:

David Baxter
Victor Brown
Aaron Clark 2nd (Doug)
Jomel Clark
Lorenzo Crumpley
Marlon Holt
Darryl Hopkins
Mike Jacobs
Demetrius Johnson
Rufus Liggans
Darren Lowman
Remel McCoy
Lamar Offield
Daryll Primm
Donald Thompson
Alvin Vann
Allen Williams
Eric Williams
Kris Woods

Darian, age 27

LONELINESS
by
Darian L. Clark

Loneliness is depression
Depression leads to death
Just because of loneliness
Someone may take his last breath

Loneliness might be divorce
Loneliness might be without a friend
But whatever loneliness means to you
It will always come back again

No one wants loneliness
But it cannot be stopped
Loneliness may be fear
Or an arrest by a cop

Loneliness may come once
But it will definitely come twice
As many times as it comes
Being lonely just isn't nice

Loneliness may be fright
Or even someone you miss
It might even be the dark
Or even a good-bye kiss

The above poem was written by Darian in 1985 at the tender age of thirteen.
Darian's life was taken on July 1, 2000, at the age of twenty-eight.

THE SHOOTING

How do you survive after half of your heart has been killed? Do you try to assure your family, your friends, and even yourself that you are still the same person you were before you experienced the loss? Do you depend on the strength of others to keep you sane and in touch with reality to keep from falling apart, or do you confess to one and all that you are not strong enough to bear the burden associated with the loss of your child and are just about ready to give up? You must, of course, stay strong and continue to function in a reasonable manner inasmuch as there are people depending on you and surely you cannot let them down. Life goes on; or does it?

On the morning of Saturday, July 1, 2000, I received a telephone call that I will never forget as long as I live, for it has changed my life drastically and forever.

I was awakened at approximately 4:45 a.m. by a gentleman who did not identify himself, but simply asked me if I was Gloria Clark. When I validated to him that I was Gloria Clark, he then asked, "Do you have a son by the name of Darian Clark?" At the mention of my son's name, I immediately jumped to my feet and in a quivering voice quietly answered, "Yes, I do." The un-welcomed voice on the other end of the phone proceeded to tell me that Darian had been involved in an accident. My first impulse was that he had been involved in an *automobile* accident, which had possibly left him with a broken bone or a few minor injuries. I tearfully asked the caller, "What has happened to him?" The following words will be etched in my mind forever. He said, "He's been shot and it's very bad. Please get here as soon as you can." "What hospital?" I managed to say in a trembling voice, as I vaguely remember. Almost before the gentleman could finish informing me he was in the emergency room of the Erie County Medical Center, I slammed the phone down and screamed to the top of my voice that Darian

9

had been shot. I have a not-so-vivid recollection of throwing on clothing and scurrying around the house much like that of a mad woman, not really knowing exactly what to do or what I would encounter once I arrived at that dreadful place. It was much like a nightmare that I was trying very hard to awaken from, but only I could not wake up. This isn't really happening to me is it? I had just seen my son Friday night when he came over to my house like he so often did. My son was fine! He was happy! He was safe! What could have possibly gone so wrong in those few short hours? How could my whole world turn upside down so quickly? Nothing like this is supposed to happen to people like us. People like us meaning good, Christian people who tried to live decent, respectable lives. This all must be a terrible mistake.

On the seemingly very long ride to where would later be referred to as my son's place of death, I remember praying to my God that he would spare my baby's life and take mine instead. I explained to him, as best I could in my frame of mind, that I had lived a full rich life but my son had only just begun to live. He had a little girl who simply adored him and most certainly he had to be there for her high school and college graduations.

Emaja' was born in November of 1996 and was my first grandchild. How happy we were to finally have become grandparents! Now who will walk her down the aisle when she marries the man of her dreams who will be lucky enough to sweep her off her feet, steal her precious heart, and vow to love and cherish her forever? These are the very special accomplishments that parents eagerly await to be a part of, especially for Daddy's little girl, so I was almost certain that God would not deprive my son of those glorious moments.

Baby Emaja,
1996

I knew I had not lived a perfect spiritual life, as no man has, but I was always a believer in the power of prayer and I put my entire being into that prayer of faith that morning knowing without a shadow of a doubt that my prayer would be heard and my son's life would be spared. After all, he was so young and so full of life, how could God be so cruel as to take him away from me so soon, when he knew what an important part he played not just in my life, but also in his daughter's, brother's and father's lives. My two sons were the best of friends. The God I knew was a caring God who could never inflict such pain on one of his humble servants. I prayed to that same God every day of my life that he would protect all of my loved ones and keep them safe from any hurt, harm or danger, seen or unseen. Surely he would not forsake me now. I was sure Darian's life would be spared but I continued to pray, and pray hard as I have never prayed before.

When I arrived at the hospital, after what seemed to be an eternity, I was first greeted at the entrance of the hospital by a Buffalo police officer, who radioed to the waiting staff of the emergency room that I had arrived. By this time, my mind was so clouded that for a split second I almost forgot where I was. Once inside the Medical Center, my eyes fixed on a gentleman in a white coat who was quickly approaching me. He asked of me, "Are you Mrs. Clark?" "Yes," I answered (almost wishing I was not Mrs. Clark). "How is my son?" I asked in tears. "I'm afraid it does not look good," the doctor said. "We have been doing all we can to save your son's life, but he was shot in the head and I don't think he's going to make it."

Who was he to speculate on my son's fate, I thought. Who was he to say my son was going to die? There was a much greater power I was relying on to spare my son's life. He was the God my parents taught me to serve many years ago and the same God I taught my sons to serve as well. He was the God who said, "Ask and it shall be given." I had asked for my son's life to be spared. What more could I do? Just show me now, Lord, what you want of me and I will do it—*anything*. You were the very one who gave my son to me twenty-eight short years ago. Why do you want him back so soon? I haven't told him yet today how very much I love him and would do anything in the world for him. What would I do without him here with me? How could I face each new day knowing that I would never see his smiling face again? What would I tell his daughter when she so lovingly asks about her father? I am fully aware of the fact that bad things happen to good people, but please God, don't take him away from me yet.

In all of this madness, I had forgotten that Darian's father Aaron had to be notified of his son's condition. How was I going to break the news to

11

him? This was his baby boy also. Darian's older brother Doug also had to be told of his brother's fate. There were so many people who loved and adored Darian and they all had to be told of this life altering tragedy, but how could I inflict such pain on them all with such terrible news? Somehow I managed to call my estranged husband first and was greeted by his voice on his answering machine prompting me to leave a message. Apparently he had already left to put in a few hours on his job as he frequently did on Saturday mornings. I then called his brother Doug and also had to leave a message, as he surely was still asleep so early in the morning. The next person that came to mind was my sister Dot, who always offered words of wisdom and was also a believer in the power of prayer. I needed her there with me at that terrible moment to comfort me and tell me that everything was going to be all right and that my son would be fine. I woke her with the horrible news and asked her to contact my minister for me because I could not for the life of me remember his telephone number. I needed him there with me also for I didn't quite know what to do at this point but I knew he would have some encouraging words for me which might help me get through this tribulation. I managed by the grace of God to get in touch with all of our loved ones, except his brother Doug who apparently had not awakened, and in what seemed like a matter of minutes, my support group was there, including, of course, my minister, Reverend William A. Bunton, Jr. Rev. Bunton was indeed a man of God who was never too busy to attend to the needs of his congregation. He was a person I could always count on in the time of trouble, but would he be able to get me through this? My sisters Dot and Betty, my niece Cynthia and my best friend Alvin were the first to arrive at the hospital, which didn't surprise me. These were the people I could depend on no matter what happened in my life. They were always there to lend their support and a shoulder to cry on! It's not that I could not depend on the rest of my family of course, because certainly I could, under any circumstances, but there is always someone special in your life who will help you bear your burdens and listen to and understand your problems like no one else can, and these were my *special* people.

As a matter of fact, my niece Cindy could very well relate to my misery and grief for she too had suffered the loss of a child. Her baby girl, Latrice Lynette, was called to glory in 1978 when she was only three years old. She died of cancer before she even began to live. I know now, if I did not know before, just how devastating her baby's death was to her. My friend Alvin was also no stranger to losing loved ones for he too had suffered several losses in his family quite recently. I'm sure my plight brought back unpleasant memories for them both, but still they were right there offering their support, trying to conceal their pain and dwelling only on mine. We all started praying for my son, everyone feeling each other's pain and all feeling so helpless but retaining our faith nonetheless.

I finally gained enough composure to ask the doctor if I could see my baby. His response was that they would "clean him up" and I could go in to see him but cautioned me about his physical appearance. The few steps I took to get to my son's room was the longest walk of my entire life. When I looked at my precious son's face, I cringed as I thought to myself that it was not the same handsome face I had seen only hours before sitting at my dining room table laughing and joking and reveling in the delight of going out with friends after a hectic week of work. "Mom, I need your car tonight," he had said. He had a car of his own but mine was in much better condition than his and anytime he was going somewhere special he would borrow mine. Of course I always allowed him to take it because I could never deny Darian anything. He could wrap me around his little finger and he knew it! Had I prevented him from taking my car that dreadful night however, would none of this had happened? I wished at that moment that I could turn back the hands of time and it would be Friday night again and that when Darian came to borrow my car I would have told him empathically, "No" and insisted on him staying home that night. Had that happened would I still be standing by his death bed? Or was this his destiny and nothing could have prevented this? I believe our destiny is predetermined at birth and I know Darian believed that also for we had discussed it on several occasions. If that is so, then some of my guilt will dissipate and this will be slightly easier for me to bear. How can I be sure, though?

I took my son's hand and held it gently in mine as I told him how very sorry I was that this awful thing had happened to him and that I loved him very much. It was almost as if he had been holding onto life awaiting my arrival, for as soon as I told him I loved him his heart stopped beating and we were rushed out of that tiny room so they could resuscitate the heart that I had given life to and that was such an integral part of me. The same heart I had carried in my womb for nine months nurturing and loving. Please God, bring him back to me!

A short while after we had been ordered to leave his room, the doctor came out and asked me if I would sign a document instructing them not to resuscitate him when his heart stopped again as surely it would. It was

13

explained to me that it would be a futile effort to keep reviving him and would only prolong his misery for they could do nothing more to save his life. He had lost a massive amount of blood and his brain had severe swelling. Clinically, my child was already gone, with only a machine breathing for him. How does one justify giving another the authority to let half of your heart die? Life is very cruel. With trembling hands, I willingly signed the document and at the same time apologized to Darian for having to do so. "I am so sorry, baby, but I have no other choice. I cannot have you suffer any longer than need be; you have already suffered enough. If I thought for one moment that there was the slightest chance for you to survive this trauma, no one in this world could force me to sign your life away. Please, please forgive me, my love!"

So it was done. Darian Lamar Clark was pronounced dead at 6:10 a.m. in the emergency room of the Erie County Medical Center on an otherwise beautiful Saturday morning, after being senselessly shot and abandoned by a deranged, cold-blooded killer. We were told by the homicide detectives that the police were making their routine rounds that morning when they saw Darian's body lying in the street. As Darian was leaving the nightclub he had gone to that evening with friends, he was approached by a young man whose intent was apparently to rob him, as he had done to someone else earlier in the evening. He pulled out a gun, aimed it at Darian and pulled the trigger. Just that simple. In a matter of seconds my youngest child was taken from me, brutally, abruptly, without reason. After the shooting, he ran like the coward he was and stayed in hiding for over a year. I'm not sure what happened to the young men Darian was out with that night, but it is my understanding that one of them sat in the street with Darian and held him in his arms until the ambulance arrived.

The doctor had told us earlier in the evening that Darian had a strong heartbeat when he was brought in, but he had lost an enormous amount of blood because no one bothered calling 911 nor did anyone attempt to get the attention of the investigating police officers as they drove past to report the incident because apparently no one cared; they just watched him lying there, dying. Just another young man gunned down on the mean east side streets of urban America. It happens almost every day so why should Saturday, July 1st be any different? The gunman did not care that Darian was my son. That demon didn't even know us. He did not care that the body he left lying in the street to die was that of someone whose life had meaning and purpose and had family that loved him dearly and cared for his well being.

My son's murder did not fit the profile of many other young men who fall victim to crime on our city streets, for he was neither a gang banger, a robber nor was he a buyer, seller or a user of drugs; so why was he a casualty to this aggression? His only purpose for being where he was that night was to have fun and socialize with his friends. He loved the nightclub atmosphere, and in a perfect world, a world without guns and illegal drugs, he would have been able to enjoy himself, wherever he went, without having to worry about his life being snuffed out. What sin could he have possibly committed to have warranted his sadistic execution at the hands of that murderer? If I knew the answer to this question, this entire nightmare might make a little more sense; but then again perhaps it wouldn't! There had been a rash of murders that summer and every time I heard of another young man getting shot and killed it saddened me deeply. I shed tears and said a prayer for their soul to be saved and for the family members who were left behind to bear the grief and pain of losing a loved one, but never once did it occur to me that my son would also end up a victim. Now perhaps someone is praying for me as I did for them.

After Darian was officially pronounced dead, we were allowed to view his body once more so we could bid our final farewell to our beloved. I remember not being able to stand at his bedside without the support of his father's arms holding me up. I felt very ill. When I looked at his swollen, bruised body and realized that I would never see my baby again, in this life, I asked myself why my Lord had forsaken me and taken away the most precious gift of all, that of life, my son's life at that! Then it suddenly dawned on me that Darian's brother had still not arrived. Oh my God, he will be devastated. We must find him! I made another attempt to reach him on his cell phone and that time I did get an answer and he said he was on his way to the hospital. Of course the first thing he wanted to know was "How's Darian?" I did not want to address that question over the phone especially while he was behind the wheel of a car, so I told him that I would tell him when he arrived, but to get there as quickly as possible. It was only a matter of minutes before the policeman guarding the emergency room entrance again radioed to the staff that my son was driving up. I hurriedly attempted to intercept him so I could break the news to him as gently as possible to avoid him having to hear such terrible news from strangers, such as the hospital personnel. I imagine the look on my face when he saw me approaching him said it all. I grabbed him and held him as tightly as I could while informing him that his brother and best friend was deceased. His agony quickly made me forget about my own pain as I concentrated primarily on his. How can a heart feel so much pain and continue to beat? His cries of sorrow saddened me so profoundly that I re-live that horrible moment almost every day of my life.

He too asked if he could see his brother one last time, as if he did not believe us and had to see for himself that he was truly gone. I pray to God that I will never have to witness such grief and pain in my son again—ever!

Doug & Darian
Family Reunion
Philadelphia, Pennsylvania, 1997

Before we left the hospital, I conferred with the doctor to see if Darian's organs could be donated to the organ bank so he could continue to live on, even in someone else's body. He was such a strong, healthy individual, I thought he could possibly save another's life and I was sure this is what he would have wanted. I was very disappointed when the doctor said it would not be possible to save any of his organs, even though they were perfectly healthy, due to the fact they had to give him an emergency blood transfusion as soon as he arrived at the hospital because he had lost so much blood, therefore not having enough time to get a sample of his own blood type. This saddened me deeply.

I was certainly not a stranger to death or the pain of suffering for I had endured the loss of loved ones before, but of course nothing of this magnitude. What could compare to the loss of your child? Losing my son brought back unpleasant memories of me losing my father many years ago. My dad passed away in 1975 and that was my first *real* experience with the agony of losing a loved one. In 1986 my niece Carolyn also passed away after a very brief illness at the age of only thirty-six. She left behind two young children who have since grown up to be beautiful, intelligent young people who are both in college in doing quite well. Only four short years after that, my great-niece Tanya was killed at the age of twenty. Tanya was a brilliant young woman with such a great future ahead of her and so much promise. She had aspirations of joining the military and accomplished that dream in 1989 when she joined the Navy a year after graduating from City Honors High School, and served in Japan for more than a year before being assigned to a San Diego Navy Base. She was a data processor in the Navy and had been selected to begin Officer Training School, but her life was taken from her before she had a chance to fulfill her dream. She was shot and killed by a Marine who had been asked to leave the club they were in because of his disorderly behavior. He later returned with a weapon and opened fire on the entire establishment wounding several people, Tanya being one of them. This loss was devastating to our family and took me a long time to recover from the shock of it all. The greatest loss I had suffered however, before now that is, was losing my sister Katie to that terrible disease called cancer. Katie passed away in 1991 and that devastated me more that anyone could ever imagine for she was not only a sister, she was also my best friend and confidante. We confided in one another about everything and did many things together and I did not see how I could ever get past the pain of losing her, but I did. Now, I am forced with yet *another* loss. One 100 times greater than any I had ever felt before. Will I also get over this one?

My son was not a perfect human being but he was a good, kind person. Everyone who knew him loved him and he indeed was a lover of life and a lover of people. I taught my sons to live and enjoy life to the fullest but always love and respect people along the way and to treat everyone the way they themselves wanted to be treated. They were brought up in the Church and knew our Lord and Savior Jesus Christ. They were baptized at an early age and were raised with morals and values and considered everyone as an equal knowing God made all men in his image. Darian was a sensitive, caring, respectful young man. His killer had devastated an entire family with this senseless, violent act. He had taken away a loving son, a grandson, a brother, a cousin, a nephew a friend and has left a four-year-old child to grow up without a father. What kind of an animal would shoot someone and leave them lying in the street to die, and why would God allow such a terrible thing to happen? Obviously the person responsible for my son's death did not know Jesus Christ as his personal Savior.

God never made mistakes and I was taught never to question his authority, but I was so confused and so terribly hurt that I needed answers and I needed them right away. "Hear my prayer, O Lord, give ear to my supplications: in thy faithfulness answer me, and in thy righteousness." I continued my quest for answers but received none, which left me more confused and more convinced that the God I knew had forsaken me. My heart was heavy, my spirit was broken and I could feel myself allowing my pain to turn to anger; anger at God for not protecting my son as I had asked him to do.

Word of Darian's demise spread very quickly and within hours after returning from the hospital, my home was overflowing with friends and relatives sharing in my grief. My son had many loyal and devoted friends who showed their love in so many ways that it touched me deeply to see how well loved he was. It made me realize that my husband and I had done a very decent job of raising our son. "May the works I've done speak for me," and the presence of so many people was quite an unspoken tribute to his character. He was loved!

The difficult task of preparing for my son's funeral was now ahead of me and I did not know how I would get through it. Parents are not supposed to bury their children; our children are supposed to make our burial arrangements. We have experienced the joys and the sorrows of life and all it has to offer whereas our children still have so much living and learning to do. It just does not seem fair that they should pre-decease their elders. But then again, life is not fair.

As I began the necessary preparations after Darian's death, I began to reminisce about his birth and the wonderful life he had. He was the second of two sons. My first son Doug (whose birth name is Aaron Douglas after his father) was born on September 26, 1969. My husband and I were such proud parents. We finally had a son; a family. We doted on Doug and gave in to his every whim, as we did also to Darian who came along on April 28, 1972.

Doug & Darian
Ages 3½ & 1

Darian could not wait to make his presence known for he was in quite a hurry to be born. He came into this world happy-go-lucky and that personality never changed. He had a smile that would melt an iceberg and believe me, he used that technique quite often to get what he wanted and it usually worked. He did not lack charm or confidence at all, in other words, Darian could melt the coldest heart. When he was a baby, his disposition was such that when he awakened from a nap, instead of the usual crying associated with babies his age, he would wake up giggling and babbling to himself as if he were in his own little world. When I walked into his room, his eyes sparkled so brightly and he grinned from ear-to-ear acknowledging my presence. How that smile melted my heart. At the age of six months, he developed a flu-like virus, which dehydrated and almost killed him. He was hospitalized for about a week and the entire hospital staff fell in love with him in that short period of time. Every time I went to visit him, I would have to search the entire hospital floor to find him because one of the nurses had him in their arms. He had a head full of black curly hair and the most beautiful eyes and long eyelashes that you ever wanted to see.

Darian had many childhood illnesses when he was growing up. He was a very sickly child who suffered with asthma and hay fever and was allergic to many things including grass and pollen, which kept him in the house many days while the other kids were outside playing. He was forever coming down with a cold which always resulted in a high fever and a trip to the doctor's office. I recall having to sit up with him almost all night sometimes comforting and nursing him back to health while trying to bring his temperature down. Perhaps this is how we became so very close, by me having to devote so much more of my time to him because he needed me much more often than his brother Doug, who, thank God, was very seldom ill. Despite his afflictions, he was still one of the happiest little boys I knew.

On his first day of school at the age of five, I remember how I hated to leave him because he had never been in the care of anyone except his loving family. Would he be treated well? Would he miss me? He cried a little the first day I left him, but after that he was fine. He adapted to his new surroundings quite comfortably and it was not long before all of his teachers simply adored him and would always tell me what a polite and respectful child he was. That came as no surprise to me though because we had raised him to be just that, polite and respectful along with all of his other loving characteristics. At an early age, he had one time said he wanted to become a fireman. He later changed that to wanting to become a telephone man like his father. As I think back now, I remember that the occupation he wanted to pursue when he grew up changed from day to day. He may have been indecisive about his career objectives but he could have been anything he wanted to be—he was a born leader.

Darian was always very small for his age. All through his high school years he was the smallest kid in his class and of course the other children would tease him about being so little. This hurt him very much, and he would come home from school some days almost in tears because of the taunting of his classmates, being so self-conscious of his height and weight. I would try to encourage him by trying to convince him that if his friends teased him and made him feel uncomfortable about his size, then they were truly not his friends at all, as true friends accept you as you are, unconditionally, and despite his dimensions he was the most perfect kid I knew. Our little chats would always lift his spirits and in time his small statue did not matter to him too much at all and he started feeling good about himself and gaining that confidence that he took with him to his early grave.

My son's small stature turned into muscle and he became quite a looker and quite the ladies man. Many of the girls he met through his high school years became infatuated with Darian and he had more friends than one could possibly imagine, male and female.

Darian, happy at age 17

My home became everyone's home and there was a steady flow of young people in and out daily, morning, noon and night. I didn't mind, however, because I usually knew where my boys were. Ninety percent of the time they were in our basement—better known as the clubhouse—entertaining their friends and doing whatever teenagers do, so I simply had very few worries as to their whereabouts.

My sons had a good life. We were very blessed and there was very little that they ever wanted and did not receive and absolutely nothing that they *needed* and did not get. Some might declare that we spoiled our sons but I prefer to think of it as merely showing them how very much they were loved and appreciated. They were not angels mind you, but we did not have any *major* problems while raising our sons. Life was good!

There was a constant flow of family and friends from morning to night, each one offering a different tale to tell about Darian. Everyone loved him so very much. The day before his funeral, I recall meeting a woman who told me that her daughter had been a very good friend of Darian's. She said that two of her sons had been shot and killed (at different times) and Darian helped her daughter get through that very tough time in her life. She said she would never forget him for that. A few of his other friends informed me that Darian, on more than one occasion, had opened his home to them when they had fallen on tough times and had no place else to go. I had others tell me that he was one of the best friends they ever had and that he would have given you the shirt off of his back if needed. These were the testimonies I heard from so many people and it did my heart good to have them reinforce what a good, kind person I knew him to be. I also received a letter from a friend of his whom I had almost forgotten about because I had not seen him in such a long time. When I read his letter it touched my heart so that I have to share it with you. He wrote:

Dear Mr. & Mrs. Clark,

How are you doing? I know it's been a long time since you've heard from me. The true reason for this letter is to send you my condolences. I'm having a hard time digesting the news about Darian. I don't want to believe it, so I can imagine the melancholy you are going through. I'm so sorry!

Your household was my role model of what a family should be like. I always wanted to be like your son, and have a mother and father like you two. I love you all and it's kind of hard to explain. I just want you to know that I'm encouraging you to be strong and know that from God we come from and to him we return! I plan to visit you when I am in town and hope I'm welcome. You're still the family I always wanted and plan to raise.

Take care of yourself and remain strong. Prepare yourself for the day of judgement! God loves you.

Love,
Bennie

I take that lovely letter out periodically and read it for encouragement. I continue to anxiously await a visit from that young man.

It was now one day before my son's funeral and the family was preparing to go to the funeral home to view his body. From the way I remembered Darian's face while he was lying so still on that tiny hospital bed, I thought for sure we would be forced to have a closed casket and no one would be able to see his handsome face one last time before we had to bid him good-bye, but the funeral director assured us that he would be presentable enough for all to see. This was the moment of truth. If he did not look like the son I had last seen less than a week prior to this tragedy then the casket would remain closed through the entire service. By the time my husband, son, and I arrived at the funeral home, I felt as if someone had put fifty-pound weights in both shoes for I could hardly walk. I was not sure what I was going to see when I went into the viewing room. Was it going to be someone I recognized and loved, or would it be a stranger I had never seen before? As we slowly entered the room and approached the beautiful casket we had picked out only days before, my heart was pounding at such an exorbitant rate that I was fearful I was going to succumb to a heart attack right there next to my son's body. When I gained the courage to look at the shell lying there, my anxiety was overcome by delight for it looked so very much like the sleeping face of the son that I had seen so many times before in the last twenty-eight years. I really do not remember how many times I thanked the funeral director for the extremely talented workmanship performed on my son to have him look so flawless in spite of the damage that bullet had done.

The tears I started to shed at that time were two-fold. First, because reality had finally set in and I knew my son had truly departed this life, as we knew it, and my life would never be the same. Second, because he looked so peaceful lying there which led me to believe that he did not suffer at the hands of his perpetrator and his soul was at peace when he left this world. That made me feel extremely comforted. Thank you again, Lord, for bringing me through yet another hurdle.

When we returned to the house, everyone was in reasonably good spirits because our son looked so perfect and peaceful. Time was quickly drawing nigh however when we would have to bid our final good-bye. He has been with me this far; would he forsake me now? What would tomorrow bring? Could I be strong for my other son, who was now my major concern? I could not fall apart now! I prayed that night for strength to get through another day. I had no idea what tomorrow would bring, but I knew I had to hold up because people were depending on me. I felt I had let Darian down by not protecting him from his killer. I couldn't let everyone else down too. I began praying again which is all that I knew to do. I had gotten this far by his grace. He can't desert me now.

When I went to bed that night, I had a dream that Darian came to me with that awesome smile on his face and told me to announce to everyone that he is still here. "I'm back.," he had said. Oh how wonderful it would have been if that were true.

Antioch Baptist Church
Buffalo, New York

THE FUNERAL

It was finally Thursday, July 6th, the day they were going to put my baby's remains in the cold, wet ground. Even though God had yet revealed to me why he took my son from me, he had helped me get through this far; would he desert me now? Getting dressed that morning was quite an effort for me, though I finally managed. I wore all white, which to me represented purity. I felt the Lord had washed Darian's soul and made it white as snow. He was with the Lord now and I could visualize him in his long, white robe in Heaven attending to the needs of the angels. The wake was scheduled to begin at 11:00 a.m. at the Antioch Baptist Church with the funeral immediately following at approximately noon. It was now about 10:30 a.m. and everyone including my minister was outside waiting for me to exit so we could have prayer before we left for the church. I was dressed, but not ready, if you can understand what I mean by that. I had known for six days that this day would befall us, but still I was not prepared for it. We had a word of prayer, entered the awaiting limousine and my husband, son, and his girl Jennifer, my mother-in-law and I were on our way to the end of my world.

The ride to the church seemed very long and quiet. A few words were uttered along the way but I really cannot remember now what was said. Does it matter? When the limousine pulled up in front of the church, there were many family members already lined up on the front steps ready to begin the processional but were awaiting our arrival. As I started to make my way toward the front steps of the church, I heard a very small familiar voice call out "Grandma!" As I turned around, from the corner of my eye I could see my adorable little granddaughter running toward me with out-stretched arms. With one leap, Emaja' was in my arms hugging my neck and clinging to me very securely. I squeezed her very tightly, tearfully realizing that she was now the only tangible thing that was left of my son for she was his precious child. As long as I have her, I thought, a part of him will live on forever for she is so much like her father and so much an essential part of me. She is such a bright child but no matter how intelligent she is, how can you make her understand what has happened to her father? Can words possibly explain to her that she will never see her father in this life again because someone murdered him? What does a four-year-old child know about the hereafter? Only in time will she understand the fate of her father and why he had to leave her at such a young age. Thank you, God, for giving her to us before you took Darian away.

As we proceeded down the aisle of the church, I thought of how many times I had previously attended a funeral in that big, old, beautiful sanctuary, but this time it was *one* of the most important people in my life lying there so still in front of the altar. Why was this happening to me? What had I done so sinful for God to inflict such pain on my family and me? Thoughts of him abandoning me raced through my head and I was almost ready to explode with sorrow. It was a very long and sad journey down that aisle. This was now the moment of truth. Can I do this? I was seated in the first seat of the first pew so I could acknowledge mourning family and friends as they marched around to view my baby's body and to offer their condolences to me. I remember thinking how fortunate those people were who still had their loved ones and selfishly wishing it was someone other than my son lying there. The church was filled to capacity with mourning friends and family. There were people there that I had not seen in years but came to town especially for this sad occasion. Everyone who spoke had something good to say about my son. Not because they thought it was the proper thing to say but because it was the truth and they meant it from the bottom of their hearts.

Being there with so many close friends and mourning family members brought back the unpleasant recollection of his cousin Toyami's funeral only two years prior in White Plains, New York. When the boys were young, they would fly there every year to spend the summer with their cousins Toyami and Jomel. How they looked forward to that trip. They were more like a sister and brothers than cousins and they just loved being spoiled by their Uncle Tom and Aunt Jackie. Spending the summers in White Plains went on for years until they outgrew that and chose to start spending the summer home, with their own friends. When Toy became ill and we told the boys that her prognosis was not good, that is the saddest I had ever seen my sons; especially Darian, who she had so lovingly nicknamed "Honey Bun" because he was her pet. We all loved her so much. She was like the daughter I never had and I could not have loved her any more if she were my own child. Only a few years prior to her death, we had attended her fairy tale wedding, where everything was so perfect and so festive and everyone couldn't have been happier.

Doug, Darian & Dad
Cousin Toyami's Wedding
White Plains, New York, 1989

It seemed like we had to turn right around and go back to that same place for her funeral. We funeralized Toyami in January of 1998 and had to travel once again in April of the same year to Chicago for the burial of my little great-nephew Michael Wayne. Michael was run down by a hit and run driver while crossing the street and left lying there, much like Darian. He was only seven years old when he was killed, just one month shy of his 8th birthday. Who would be so cruel as to do something so dreadful? Doesn't anyone care anymore? Is everyone so unsympathetic that they have no compassion and no regard for a human life? This is the state our world is in now and it is not a pleasant place to dwell. His killer is still at large and I hope that every day of his life he is tormented by the sight of that baby he left lying there and that he has endless suffering for taking that child's life. Life's a maze of twists and turns though, and you just never know what's around the next corner. Perhaps his killer has met with a fate worse than what he imposed on little Michael. Wouldn't that be poetic justice?

The thought of all of my deceased loved ones flashed in my mind as I was laying my son to rest and I just wanted it all to end. No more pain, Lord, please!

It, of course, was a very sad funeral, as funerals are. I was in a daze during the entire service knowing that once we left the church, we would be escorting my son, my baby, to his final resting place. No one in that huge, beautiful church could have imagined the pain that was surging through my entire body while I was sitting there trying so hard to be strong. It's a feeling that has no description and that I hope I will never, ever have to experience again. Reverend Bunton preached a very refined eulogy, which was short and sweet. I cannot really remember now what he said, but I do remember at the time thinking how appropriate it was. He was a very kind individual who cared so deeply for his congregation and all young people in general. I had been a member of his church for many years and never once had I called on him for inspiration or support or spiritual guidance when he did not make himself available to me. He was never too busy to counsel or offer his services to anyone whenever needed. You did not have to be a member of his congregation for him to lend his support and prayers. He is a good man.

Darian looked very boyish and so at rest lying there in his gorgeous ocean-blue casket, which had a cross and the words "IN GOD'S HANDS" inscribed on the inside of the shiny sky-blue crepe liner, surrounded by all of the beautiful flowers. Blue was his favorite color, so his friends had gone through his wardrobe and picked out a dark blue collarless shirt and a pair of beige dress pants for his grand finale, for that's the way he would have wanted it. We had attended our family reunion in 1999 in Chicago, Illinois which was hosted by my oldest sister Ann and her family (It was her grandson that was killed by the hit and run driver) and the boys had such a good time that weekend I requested that the T-shirt he had purchased during that trip, be worn under his dress shirt, so he would never forget the fun time he had. That was the last trip we had together as a family and they had a ball that weekend!

Darian was not a suit and tie person, but very casual. As a matter of fact, casual dress was the attire of all of the young people that morning. There were mini skirts, tank tops, backless dresses and slits up to the thigh. So many young people were wearing custom-made T-shirts with Darian's picture imprinted on the front, which were a final tribute to his memory. They gave him the send off he definitely would have chosen had he been able to request it himself.

It had rained momentarily that morning so the ground at the cemetery was a little moist but not soaking wet. Almost everyone who was at the church also came to the cemetery to bid him one last good-bye. I was so relieved that the caretakers did not lower his casket while we were in the cemetery because I think seeing them do that would have taken me right over the edge, watching them put him in the cold ground. Knowing they were going to do that was one thing but watching them do it was yet another. I could not have handled that at all. Words were expressed, flowers were placed, tears were shed and then it was all over. A time to be born; A time to plant; A time to build; A time to love; A time to die. We gave him a spectacular home going that day. I never shortchanged him in life and I was not about to do it in death. Thank you, sweet Jesus, for getting me through one of the most difficult days of my entire life.

Later that evening, my home was still overflowing with grief-stricken family and friends who sat around reminiscing and telling stories of some of the funny things Darian used to do and say. He was quite the comedian, always making jokes and always so upbeat. The good memories of him will have to keep him alive in our hearts now, and I have so many good memories that will remain with me. He was a good son, a good brother and a good friend. Not once did Darian ever disrespect me like so many other young people tend to do with their parents. He always humbled himself to me and had an uncanny way of making *me* feel bad for yelling at him. I never wanted him to be angry with me and he rarely was, nor was I with him. He wanted so very badly to make me proud of him and he tried so hard to do so, and I was proud of my son; both of my sons. I took pride in being a mother and a friend to my family and didn't find parenting difficult at all. That's the *one* thing I'd like to think I was really good at, being a mother; a good mother! They were my whole life; my world, and there was absolutely nothing I would not have done for either of them and they knew that. We had a very special mother/son bond, which could never have been broken. Until now that is. It's almost as if he is still here with me because I cannot admit to myself that he is gone. It's like a nightmare that I will soon awaken from and see Darian running up my stairs yelling "Hey, Momma, it's your son. Anybody home?"

I know I must face the fact that I will never hear that phrase coming from his lips ever again, nor will I ever again see or hear him run in my home being silly like he often did. I will never have the opportunity to send him another greeting card on his birthday or another joke or e-mail which we so often did. Darian had become quite computer literate and we would communicate via the internet quite frequently. As a matter of fact, I recall the last e-mail I sent to my son. Someone had sent me a story via the internet about a little boy who was born without ears. All through his school years he was teased and humiliated which resulted in him being very self-conscience of himself and not having many friends. His mother felt the pain her son was in and told him that she was looking for a donor for him, someone who would donate him a pair of ears. Well one day his mother approached him so happy she could hardly speak and informed him that she had found a donor. This made the young boy very happy. Once he had his ears his whole life changed. His grades in school improved greatly, he had a multitude of friends and became a huge success in life. Over the years his mother became ill and eventually passed away. As he and his father were standing over his mother's casket saying their final good-bye's, his father said, "Son, did you ever wonder why your mother let her hair grow so long through the years and never cut it? The son obviously had never really thought about it until his father pulled his mother's long flowing hair back to reveal the fact that she had no ears. She had been the "secret" donor who had so unselfishly given her precious son her ears. This story touched my heart so because it demonstrated the strength of a mother's love. The author of this story must have been a mother herself to have captured, so uniquely the power of a mother's love. I e-mailed this story to Darian with a little note illustrating the fact that there was nothing stronger than a mother's love for her child and letting him know that I would have done the same for him. I told him that I loved him so much that I would have gladly given my ears, my life even for him if I had to. Darian responded to my letter by telling me, "Mom, that was a beautiful story and it brought tears to my eyes. I know you would do anything in the world for me, but what you may not realize is that I would do the same for you. I love you very much, Mom."

That was the last communication between my son and me. Maybe that was our way of telling each other good-bye and didn't even know it. Oh God how I miss those little things. If only I could see and talk to him one more time this is probably what I would say to him:

My Dearest Darian,

From the moment I conceived you, my son, I knew you were going to be someone very special. When you were born, after holding you in my arms for the first time and checking you over from head to toe and counting all of your little fingers and toes, I thanked God once again for giving me yet *another* perfect child.

When I was feeding you, breathing for you and nurturing you in my womb, I was able to keep you safe, my love. From the day you took your first breath on your own, I still tried so very hard to protect you. Believe me, Darian, I did everything in my power to guard you from one of the very elements that eventually ended up taking you away from me so abruptly. I am so very sorry, my son, that I was not able to shield you from the terrible act inflicted upon you, which drained all of the life out of your body. If I could have taken your place, I would have done so a dozen times or more. In your much-too-brief life, you spread so much joy to so many people. Everyone who knew you loved you. I too loved you so very, very much, my son, but God loved you more. You are now in his garden with all of the other beautiful flowers and I am waiting for the day when I will see you again. Remember all of the jokes and the funny stories you will have to tell me, for when I get there, I want to hear everything. We will have a lot of catching up to do.

Well, my baby, I'm not going to tell you good-bye. I will merely say "See ya Butchie," because one day I will. Rest in peace, my Angel, until we meet again. Oh, and by the way "Butchie," thank you so much for being my son and my friend. Until we meet again, my precious son.

Love,
Mom

I will lift up mine eyes unto the hills, from whence cometh my help; My help cometh from the Lord which made heaven and earth.
—Psalms 121: 1-2

The "Building"

LIFE GOES ON

In August 1994, my husband's father had passed away and left the three-bedroom home he was living in to my husband Aaron and his only brother Tom. Since they both already owned their own home, they unanimously agreed to transfer the property to Darian and his brother Doug. The boys were very excited about moving out on their own, and so was I. They needed the responsibility of taking care of themselves, and not having Mom around to cater to them (as I had become so used to doing), would be good for them. This would be quite a learning experience for them both. Late in 1994, the two brothers and their friend Kris moved into the grandfather's house, also referred to as the bachelor pad. I remember how excited we were decorating the apartment and each one adding their own personal touch to make it special. It was quite pleasing to the eye when we had completed the decorating and it was not long before it too became everyone's hang-out. They referred to it simply as the "building." It was during this period that Darian acquired the nickname "Butchie." How they arrived at that name I have no idea, but I too began calling him that! That name really suited him for some reason. My sons had good times and they also had a few bad times living on their own, but each episode made them stronger and less dependent on their father and me.

After Darian's death, I had to force myself to enter that apartment, for this time it was not for the joy of decorating it for a new beginning, but for the sorrow of having to remove all of his personal belongings for the end had come. Darian's whole life was in that apartment. There were so many memories there, some good, some bad. How he had loved being on his own and having his very own place where he was the *boss*. He had become very mature and very independent, which I could see developing more and more each day by him being away from Mom. Removing his life from that apartment was not an easy task, but the Lord once again gave me the strength I needed to get through it. I gave most of his belongings away to anyone who wanted them, with the exception of a few of his sweaters, which I kept for myself to wear around the house. You wouldn't believe all of *my* dishes and silverware I found in his apartment from when he would come over my house and eat on the run taking my dishes with him! I, however, didn't mind a bit! He knew that anything I had belonged to him and his brother as well. When we had finished moving everything out of his apartment and returned home, I remember crying myself to sleep that night while holding onto one of his sweaters, which was all that was left of my son. I knew all too well that my life would never be the same.

I tried to stay in touch with the homicide chief who was handling Darian's case to keep abreast of the progress they were making in locating his killer. I knew I would never have peace of mind until this demon was taken off the street and locked away forever. When I talked to the chief, he told me the investigation was moving along very well and his detectives had done an excellent job in almost bringing the case to a close. He assured me he had witnesses and sufficient evidence found at the scene of the crime, which would lead them to the perpetrator. All they were waiting for now was a date to take the evidence to the Grand Jury for an indictment for they knew the name of the killer. Every time I talked to him this is what I was told and then I started to question whether or not they were doing all they could do. The chief assured me of closure soon and urged me to be patient, so that's what I did; I remained patient and prayerful.

Darian's friends continued to visit my son Doug and me and life goes on, although it is not quite the same and *we* are not quite the same. I have mixed emotions when I see his friends, however. I am always very glad to see them of course because they are all like my own children, but there is also a little sadness because seeing them makes me wish for Darian even more. They stop by periodically to check on me to make sure I am all right. I always tell them that I am, but deep down inside I know, and I think they also know that I will never be all right again.

If they only knew how often I lock myself in my room and cry uncontrollably because the pain is still so very intense. Or how often I cry myself to sleep at night wishing I could bring my son back. If Darian could come back, I doubt very seriously if he would want to return to this cruel, evil world though. I know he is in a much better place because he has come to me on several occasions to let me know that he is doing just fine. Everyone tells me that the pain will lessen in time but I can't see that happening any time soon.

Well, it was now Labor Day and no arrest has been made. The last time I spoke with the chief of the homicide bureau I was told again that they were still waiting for the Grand Jury date so they could get an indictment. I then called the assistant District Attorney who confirmed his story. When are they going to arrest this demon? What's wrong with our justice system, I thought? Why can't they catch this maniac? What will it take to get him off the streets? I tried to exercise my faith in the chief and his detectives so all I could do was continue to wait, hope and pray for closure.

We had an enjoyable Labor Day with good food and good friends, despite the inclement weather. It was during this time that Dave, a good friend of my slain son filled me in on street rumors regarding his murder. He informed me that he had heard that Darian was shot by accident and the shooter did not mean to fire the gun. I truly wanted to believe his death *was* an accident because I didn't want to believe that anyone hated my son enough to purposely want him dead, but I was having a difficult time believing this story. Innocent, rational people don't walk the streets with a loaded gun, point it at someone, pull the trigger and say it's an accident. Accidents like that just do not happen. Whether it was an accident or a indiscriminate act of violence, however, the point is my son's killer is still at large and may possibly hurt or kill someone else. He must be apprehended.

When I woke up the next morning, I looked out of my bedroom window and the first thing I saw was Darian's car parked in front my house which had not been there the night before. It was there because I had sold it to my nephew Zack who was having some repairs done on it at my house. When I saw his car, for a split second, and only for a split second, I thought Darian was here again. What a jolt that was to my system. I became so hysterical and so overcome with emotion that I had to call my grief counselor for I had to share that agonizing moment with someone and release all the pain I was feeling by talking it out. I was in such bitter pain that morning that I seriously contemplated ending my own life because I did not see how my heart could withstand such torment. As those desperate thoughts raced through my head, the first person that came to my mind was my son Doug. His pain was just as great as mine and I could not add to his misery by being selfish enough to take my own life. He had already lost his brother and his best friend. He should not have to endure any more suffering on my account. My second thought was that the only sin God does not forgive you for is the taking of your own life, so therefore had I done such a horrendous thing I would never see Darian again. That thought frightened me to no extent. Once I was able to talk to someone impartial about those awful feelings, the pain lessened somewhat and I was able to function again, barely. I hope I do not experience many more days like that one.

I've finally gained the fortitude after more than two months to pick out Darian's grave marker. I went to several places before I finally found the perfect one. It is a jet-black granite-flushed marker with his picture carved into it. Very elegant! Nothing was ever too good for my son. They will not be able however, to lay his marker until next spring when the weather breaks. I was hoping it would be much sooner than that! Yet another disappointment! I have been to the cemetery on numerous occasions to talk to him and tell him how much I miss him. Maybe in time my pain will lessen, but today it is still as intense as it was the day he was killed. God took my son for a reason and perhaps I will never know what that reason is but I know I must be strong and accept it. I am trying very, very hard to accept my fate but sometimes it does seem insufferable.

It's been almost three months since my son was murdered and today I finally received a bit of good news. I called the homicide chief again (I wasn't going to let them forget about this case) and he told me that they had assigned a new district attorney to Darian's case and he gave me his number to call, which I did of course. He told me that within the next week his case would be presented to the Grand Jury and possibly a week after that, there would be a warrant issued for his arrest. That was the most encouraging information I had received in months. He instructed me to call him back in a week and he would have more information for me. That was a very long week of waiting and anticipation for me.

On the morning of October 6th, I called the district attorney again and he told me that he had good news for me which was not on public record yet, but the case had finally been presented to the Grand Jury. He said he would be able to give me more information the following week, but did say that he had a very solid case and insisted I call him back the following week. On the morning of October 10th when I called back he was able to tell me that they had issued a warrant for the arrest of Darian's killer but was not sure now where he was at this time. According to the homicide chief, this guy has a very lengthy arrest record and he was sure he would surface very soon. During my conversation with the district attorney, I discovered however that no one had been able to give a reason as to why that young man had murdered my son. There was no apparent reason for Darian to die. None of the witnesses could understand what had provoked the killer. It was suggested that he was either high on drugs or just out to prove what a big man he was by killing someone. A sick world we live in, isn't it?

I had a dream about Darian the other night. I dreamed that he had come back to us proclaiming he had dug himself out of his grave, saying, "They couldn't keep me in there." We were all so very pleased when we saw him. Our "Butchie" was back. That made me oh so happy for just a brief moment, until I awakened and realized it was only a dream and that my "Butchie" had not come back to me at all. I started that day on the downside and went into a minor state of depression, which I had done so many times before. Will this grief and pain ever dissipate?

More than four months have passed and we are celebrating Thanksgiving without one of our beloved. On November 19th, Emaja', Darian's daughter, celebrated her fourth birthday without her daddy's presence. She asks about him every time I see her and it saddens me so when she asks me why that man shot her daddy. I try to explain to her that there are bad people in this world who like to hurt other people for sometimes no reason at all. What can I really say to make her understand?

I tried so very hard to remain focused on giving thanks for my many blessings and not dwelling on the fact that "Butchie" would not be joining us for dinner. I recall that in past happier years, I would always cook an overabundance of goodies so he could pack up half of the leftovers to take home with him. The only time I was sure he was eating nourishing meals was when he dined at my house, and it would give me such great pleasure to see him eat and enjoy my cooking. Holidays were always so special in my home. We laughed and talked an awful lot when we were together and just enjoyed each other's company to the fullest. Oh how I enjoyed holidays and having my whole family together.

"Butchie" would always be the last one to arrive because he was always so busy doing other things. We used to tease him all the time about never being on time. He would give us that famous grin, make some excuse for being late and commence eating and savoring every fork-ful. The party never really started until he arrived. He was such a character! I gave thanks for my family standing around my dining room table, and for all of my other blessings, but could not complete my prayer of thanks before I was overcome with grief and pain once again! When I retired that night, he was so heavy on my mind that I had a dream about him, *again*. I could see his smiling face surrounded by light and he took his hand and placed it in mine and I squeezed it very gently (much like I had done in the emergency room that awful night). This time however it was as soft as a baby's hand and I remember smiling then myself and thinking how very happy I was because he was at peace. I think that was his way of showing me that he was going to be all right and I shouldn't worry about him! There was a sweet, sweet spirit in that place that night and I slept like a baby waking up the next morning feeling better than I had in a very long time.

Before I realized it, Christmas was here. The first time in twenty-eight years that I would have to celebrate my favorite holiday with one of my sons not being present. I had lost my Christmas spirit of course and did not even have the tenacity to decorate my home as I had done every year in the past. I didn't even put up a Christmas tree or cook dinner. It was a very somber day for me. All I did all day long was lay around and I guess you might maintain that I just felt sorry for myself. The true meaning of Christmas, I'm ashamed to say, escaped me, and the fact that it was Christ's birthday, unfortunately did not enter my mind. I was too busy drowning in my own sorrow and becoming more and more depressed to realize how much I had to be thankful for. The highlight of my day was when my son, Jennifer, Anai, Emaja' and her mom Nikki came over to exchange gifts. My granddaughters could brighten my day no matter how bleak!

I cried myself to sleep again that night! I am going through the roughest period of my entire life right now taking one day at a time. I know I will never forget my son, but I hope I will be able to get on with my life soon as this burden lessens. I can never get a closure to this nightmare however until my son's killer is apprehended and locked behind bars forever. Despite the pain I feel, I still, nevertheless count my blessings every day of my life for there is always something to be thankful for. I still have my son Doug and my two beautiful grand daughters who bring such joy into my life. I also still have my strong family, who are with me every step of the way, encouraging me and praying for and with me. When I am feeling at my lowest and think things cannot get any worst than they are or my pain cannot become any greater than it is, I begin to dwell on what I *have* and not what was taken from me. These are the important things that really matter now and that keeps me going from day to heartbreaking day.

More than five months have passed without an arrest and I am getting very anxious. I gathered all of the details of Darian's murder and sent it in to America's Most Wanted pleading for their assistance in locating my son's killer. They replied, saying they would air his story in February or March 2001. It is now early March and I have heard nothing from them. What more can I do to bring my son's murderer to justice? I have tried everything short of searching for him myself. Please Lord, let him be found soon!

Well...my persistence has finally paid off. On Saturday, August 11, 2001 my son's murderer was profiled on America's Most Wanted TV program. They presented a brief synopsis of Darian's murder and showed a picture of Darian and the perpetrator. I believe that show played a major part in the capture of my son's killer for twelve days after the program aired, on Thursday, August 23, 2001 my son's murderer was apprehended only a few blocks from the shooting, after being on the run for more than thirteen months. He was arraigned the following day and that is when I was able to look my son's killer in the face for the first time. My eyes were fixed on him during the entire proceedings while trying to figure out what is in the mind of a murderer and what makes him take someone's life. If I had the power that morning to end his life like he did my son's, I probably would have tried, but then I would not have been any better than he. No one will ever know the different emotions I was fighting that day. The tears I shed then were tears of joy; joy that he was finally behind bars where he belonged; locked up like the animal I considered him to be.

He went before the Judge on July 23, 2002 (more than two years after the murder) and he pled guilty to the highest count of the indictment, murder in the second degree. He also pled guilty to a count concerning a robbery for that was his intent that night; he was looking for someone to rob. His attorney, when asked by the Judge if he had anything to say on behalf of the defendant replied:

"Yes your Honor. I've had an opportunity to review the pre-sentence report and also was able to submit to the court a letter from my client in which he indicates his true regret and apologies and knowing that nothing he says will ever make up the loss to the family, however certainly I think from his actions he has at least demonstrated some remorse with regard to this case, just by not asking to go to trial and sparing the family the pain in accepting his responsibility for causing the death. I have nothing further to add."

· How dare he, I thought? The reason he did not go to trial was not to spare my feelings but to reduce his sentence by taking the plea bargain. Who was he trying to fool? I had absolutely no sympathy for him at all for as far as I was concerned, he could remain in jail forever and the world would be a

43

much better place. I was of course hoping they would throw the book at him and give him the maximum sentence allowed by law. That though, unfortunately did not happen!

The Judge then asked the defendant if he had anything to say in his own behalf before the court imposed sentence on him. I had been waiting for two years to hear the answer to this because at this point I still did not understand the reason for the shooting. Maybe now I can get an answer to my question. Why?

"Yes," he answered. "I just want to say that I am truly sorry for what I have done and all the pain I have caused Darian Clark's family, as well as my family, and I pray that Darian Clark's soul rests in peace. I am sorry because I have disappointed a lot of people by doing something so selfish and foolish and pray every night for my sins. I also want Darian Clark's family to know that what happened that night was not his fault and had nothing to do with him. I am not trying to make any excuses, but I was not in the right state of mind that night because of alcohol. If I had been in the right state of mind, I truly know for a fact that none of this would have happened. I want his family to know, especially his mother and father to know that my prayers are always with him no matter what happened, and I am truly sorry. I also want to say sorry to my mother and father because they raised me very well and what I did that night, truly broke their hearts. I also want to say that I am sorry to God for hurting one of his children. I pray that someday in the future I can be forgiven for all the pain I have caused everybody."

That was an extremely touching confession, wasn't it? I wonder how much of it he truly meant. People will do and say anything to save themselves. First of all I do not think I could ever find it in my heart to forgive this young man, for he committed the ultimate sin. The only sin worse than taking someone's life is the taking of your own life which is a sin you will never be forgiven for. Even the bible says "Thou shalt not kill; and he that kills shall not have forgiveness in this world, nor in the world to come." "And he that killeth any man shall surely be put to death" Lev. 24:17. I have always been opposed to the death penalty however, until now that is.

After he had finished his rehearsed speech, the Judge then spoke and said:

"Yes, well, this was a very senseless killing, cutting short a young man's life for no apparent reason, and we know that you are apologetic. I have received the letter that you wrote and you have also stated in court, and realized that what you did was wrong. But there has to be serious consequences for needless violence like this, and as you have already pointed out, your regrets can't bring this person back to life and to those that love him. As concerns your conviction for the crime of murder in the second degree, a class A felony, it's the judgment of this court that you are sentenced to an indeterminate sentence of imprisonment which shall have a maximum term of the remaining years of your natural life, and the court hereby imposes a minimum term of fifteen years. As concerns your conviction for the crime of robbery in the first degree, a class B violent felony, it's the judgement of this court that you are sentenced to a determinate sentence of imprisonment which shall have a term of fifteen years. These sentences are to run concurrently with each other. You are directed to provide a blood sample for DNA testing to be included in the DNA identification index."

At that point, he was removed from the court room and taken to the New York State Department of Correctional Services where he was to begin a *mere* fifteen-year prison sentence for the murder of my baby boy. I, however, have been sentenced to life; life without my precious son.

My mother became ill and passed away on July 22, 2003 and my nephew Mike who was serving in Iraq was killed in October of 2003 when the jeep he was riding in ran over a home made bomb near Baghdad. Twice again I was attending the funeral of a loved one at The Antioch Baptist Church. Both funerals of course brought back more unpleasant memories of my son's funeral which was held there only three short years prior. My grief was for him as well as for them.

My mom had lived a full rich life and was ninety-eight years old at the time of her death. Her parents named her Omega, for in the book of Revelation, 22:13 Jesus said, "I am Alpha and Omega, the beginning and the end, the first and the last" and she was the last survivor of five sisters and four brothers. She was a very wise woman who it seemed knew the answer to everything and had made a promise to the Lord that she would serve him for the rest of her life, and she did. I could always call on her for spiritual guidance for she was a God-fearing woman who taught her children about the power of prayer and the love of God. She had eleven children (of which I am the youngest) and would usher us all into church every Sunday morning. Going to church was not an option for us; this was mandatory. We had absolutely no choice in the matter. Her teachings helped all of her children and grandchildren to be good Christian hearted individuals. "Train up a child in the way he should go: and when he is old, he will not depart from it." Prov. 22:6. That is the way I tried to raise my sons, through her teachngs.

In my community, the death rate continues to rise and young men are being gunned down daily, many without provocation. Something must be done to rid our streets of the guns, the drugs and the thugs. Our youth are being "snatched" from us way too soon and it is time to end the violence and love and respect one another. It is time to spare another mother the agony of losing her child. We are living in an age where it is no longer safe to leave the comfort of your home to walk to the corner store and back without the fear of being killed. Love thy neighbor is a thing of the past, but we must get Christ back in our lives and teach our children the value of life and the meaning of love. Lets teach them that God is love and anyone who lives in love is living with God and God is living in him. Until we instill these values in our children, the violence will continue and there will be more blood spilled on our streets. The parents of the young man who murdered my son did not attend any of the court proceedings on their sons' behalf. Them not being by their sons' side when he needed them the most, led me to believe that he was the product of an uncaring, unloving, non-Christian home, which we are faced with much too often in our society where the end result is tragedy. Families torn apart and hearts broken because we don't have Christ in our lives. Something went very wrong in that young man's life which compelled him to take out his frustration and anger on someone he did not even know. Had Christ been a factor in his young life, perhaps my son would still be alive today for we know that all things work together for good to them that love God .

I am still struggling with my son's death and every day is a challenge for me for I miss Darian every time I breathe. It has been almost four years since my son was taken from me, but sometimes it seems like only yesterday, and "No," God has still not revealed to me why he chose Darian, but I know it was part of his Master Plan and I must accept it without question mindful of the fact that he would not put any more on me than I could bear. I try very hard to concentrate on what I have and not what I have lost. I have weathered the storm, faced my adversity and my commitment to God is greater nowthanthan it ever has been. I still have Doug and my precious granddaughters who I try to spend as much time with as possible. Emaja' is now seven and a half years old and Doug's daughter Anai Dariana (named after her uncle Darian) is seven (there is only a seven-month age difference). They are my sunshine.

Emaja, age 7

Anai, age 6½

I am no longer seeing a grief counselor and I just take one day at a time and try extremely hard not to falter in my faith as I did when my son was killed. I think back now on how I tried to "ignore" God because I thought he had deserted me when I needed him the most, when in reality he was with me every step of the way. When I thought I could not take another step, he was there holding me up to keep me from falling. I could not have made it through without him and I thank him every day for not leaving me alone to bear that heavy burden. He was with me when I thought I was not able to face another day. He was with me the many nights I cried myself to sleep. He was with me through every obstacle I faced and I was too distressed to recognize it. He was even with me when I stopped going to church because I said "What's the use?" He was there with me to direct me back to where I needed to be. The one pair of footprints in the sand was not mine, walking alone, but his, carrying me. When he promised me he would never leave me alone he meant it.

I still have the support of my family whom I continue to call on periodically and I still have Darian's friends who are concerned with my well being and check on me from time to time but less often than before. Everyone is moving on with their lives now and trying to forget the past and dwell only on the future.

To all of Darian's loyal and devoted friends, I would like to say "Thank you" for making his short life here on earth so enjoyable and truly wonderful. He loved you all very much as you did him which I witnessed every day and especially in our time of sorrow. I will never forget your acts of kindness bestowed upon my family and me when we needed you the most.

To the grieving mothers who have lost a child, joy *does* comes in the morning. You may think now that life is not worth living but strive to concentrate on the positive things in your life and try enormously hard not to let your grief consume you as I almost did. You will never forget, but it will get easier as time goes by. I still cry for my son at times and I think I always will.

As for the young man who killed my son, the scriptures are telling me that I must forgive you for the pain and suffering you put me through, but my heart is not ready to do that right now. I have read Matthew 6: 14 & 15 which states, "For if ye forgive men their trespasses, your heavenly Father will also forgive you. But if ye forgive not men their trespasses, neither will the Father forgive your trespasses." Perhaps in time, when I emerge from this *emotionally* dark place I am stuck in right now, I will find the compassion

I need to offer forgiveness to you, my enemy, which might bring a sense of closure to my life…but that hasn't happened yet! Your careless actions that night destroyed a loving family, for life as we knew it will never be the same. My one purpose in life; the one thing I enjoyed more than anything in this world, and the one thing I found so gratifying, was the joy of motherhood. You took half of that joy away from me on July 1, 2000 and I pray that every day of your life you are tortured by your despicable actions and that you see Darian's smiling face *daily* as a reminder to you of what love looks like, for surely you are clueless.

Yes, half of my heart died on July 1st, 2000, but God with his infinite wisdom and grace has continued to shower me with his blessings by allowing me to hold onto and to cherish more than ever, the remaining half; my other son Doug. I pray that God will continue to bless him and keep him safe! I love you, my son.

Mom & Doug
Doug received his Associate's Degree in Electronics
from ITT Technical Institute in 1998

A time to weep and a time to laugh;
A time to mourn and a time to dance;
A time to cast away stones and a time to gather stones together;
A time to embrace and a time to refrain from embracing;
A time to get and a time to lose;
A time to keep and a time to cast away;
A time to rend and a time to sew;
A time to keep silent and a time to speak;
A time to love and a time to hate;
A time of war and a time of peace.

REST IN PEACE, MY SON

Darian Lamar Clark, age 28
April 28, 1972 - July 1, 2000